S·B·I
SMALL BUSINESS INSTITUTE

Advanced Word Processing Simulation

Second Edition

Ann Ambrose, Dean

Business, Public Services, and Technologies
Tidewater Community College
Portsmouth, VA

Dorothy L. R. Jones, Ph.D.

Associate Vice President of Academic Affairs
Norfolk State University
Norfolk, VA

THOMSON

SOUTH-WESTERN

Australia · Canada · Mexico · Singapore · Spain · United Kingdom · United States

THOMSON

™

SOUTH-WESTERN

SBI: Small Business Institute, Advanced Word Processing Simulation, 2nd edition

Ann P. Ambrose, Dorothy L. R. Jones

VP/Editorial Director:
Jack W. Calhoun

VP/Editor-in-Chief:
Karen Schmohe

Acquisitions Editor:
Jane Phelan

Project Manager:
Diane Durkee

VP/Director of Marketing:
Carol Volz

Marketing Manager:
Mike Cloran

Marketing Coordinator:
Georgianna Wright

Production Editor:
Diane Bowdler

Production Manager:
Tricia Boies

Manufacturing Coordinator:
Charlene Taylor

Copyeditor:
Tom Lewis

Production House:
Electro Publishing

Art Director:
Michelle Kunkler

Cover Designer:
Kim Torbeck/Imbue Design
Cincinnati, OH

Cover Images:
© Getty Images, Inc.

Internal Designer:
Kim Torbeck/Imbue Design
Cincinnati, OH

Printer:
Banta
Harrisonburg, VA

COPYRIGHT © 2005
by Thomson South-Western, a part of
the Thomson Corporation. Thomson,
the Star logo, and South-Western are
trademarks used herein under license.

Printed in the United States of America
    3 4 5 07 06 05

Book ISBN: 0-538-43754-5
Book/CD ISBN: 0-538-43755-3

ALL RIGHTS RESERVED.

No part of this work covered by the
copyright hereon may be reproduced or
used in any form or by any
means—graphic, electronic, or
mechanical, including photocopying,
recording, taping, Web distribution or
information storage and retrieval
systems—without the written
permission of the publisher.

For permission to use material from this
text or product, submit a request online
at www.thomsonrights.com.

For more information
contact South-Western,
5191 Natorp Boulevard,
Mason, Ohio, 45040.
Or you can visit our Internet site at:
http://www.swlearning.com.

Round out your course with other products from South-Western!

The Candidate 2E

This beginning word processing simulation puts students to work for mayoral candidate William Wright. It is designed to develop word processing skills as students complete such tasks as formatting letters, memos, tables, press releases, and reports. Composition, critical-thinking, and decision-making skills are also developed.

Simulation *(softcover, 2-color, 128 pages)* 0-538-43757-X

River Oaks Centre 5E

An intermediate-level simulation that can be used after one semester of keyboarding, *River Oaks Centre* provides a way for students to apply and reinforce keying and document-formatting skills as part-time employees of a shopping mall. It brings keyboarding and document processing skills together with other business skills so that students can experience everyday occurrences in an actual business setting.

Simulation *(softcover, 2-color, 128 pages)* 0-538-43449-X

Ozark Zoological Park: A Word Processing Simulation 2E

This intermediate-level simulation combines the appeal of international business with a review of basic keyboarding and word processing skills. Zoo activities focus on customer service, international markets, and international shipping processes.

Simulation *(softcover, 2-color, 128 pages)* 0-538-43951-3

Integrated Business Projects 2E

This one-semester, project-based simulation lets students experience the excitement of working for a whitewater-rafting business while developing computer skills. *Integrated Business Projects* reviews the beginning, intermediate, and appropriate advanced competencies of Microsoft Office®.

Simulation *(hardcover, side spiral, 4-color, 308 pages)* 0-538-72762-4

Sports Connection 2E

This project-based, integrated simulation reinforces essential applications skills for Office XP. It provides students unique opportunities to go beyond the basics as they apply creativity in solving problems, analyzing and managing information, and using features such as Autodialer, graphs, sound files, and more.

Simulation *(softcover with CD, 2-color, 144 pages)* 0-538-72765-9

THOMSON
SOUTH-WESTERN

Join us on the Internet at www.swlearning.com

Contents

Introduction

Job Documents

Introduction

OVERVIEW OF THE SIMULATION

SBI is an advanced word processing simulation designed to reinforce your word processing skills as well as composing, critical thinking, and decision-making skills in a realistic environment.

Objectives

In this simulation, your objectives are to:

- use advanced word processing features such as merge, sort, columns, graphics, formulas, macros, and table of contents.
- format and process documents such as letters, memos, reports, tables, programs, newsletters, flyers, and outlines.
- retrieve and edit stored files.
- work from a variety of inputs.
- compose documents, think critically, and make decisions.
- create and use templates and electronic forms.

Job instructions are in the form of e-mails, faxes, and handwritten notes. Some documents are already keyed and you will simply edit them. To assist you even further, a Reference Manual contains information such as a list of the data files, a summary of software commands, sample documents, and a correlation of the simulation to Microsoft® Word competencies.

The simulation also provides you with an opportunity to create an electronic or hard copy portfolio of your work. The purpose of the portfolio is to display the different types of documents that you are capable of preparing. If you create a hard copy, you may want to store the documents in a three-ring binder with clear plastic page protectors. A copy of your resume should also be included in your portfolio. A special icon (💼), indicates a document that should be displayed in your portfolio. You will be able to use this portfolio when you go on actual interviews for jobs requiring word processing skills. Your instructor will give you more information on this portion of the simulation.

Key Features

Some of the key features of this simulation are that it:

- reinforces advanced word processing skills such as merge, sort, columns, and formulas.
- uses desktop publishing features.
- uses software reference tools such as the spell checker, thesaurus, and grammar checker.
- provides optional jobs and a test in the *Instructor's Manual.*
- includes entrepreneurship and e-commerce concepts.
- provides for the integration of academic skills.
- provides an opportunity to develop a personal resume.
- encourages saving sample documents for an electronic portfolio.

ABOUT SBI

SBI (Small Business Institute) is a private, non-profit business advocacy organization in Raleigh, North Carolina, that provides support to small businesses that have the potential to expand. It provides management and technical assistance, private and public sector referrals, one-on-one marketing, and financial and international counseling to existing and start-up businesses. In short, SBI assists firms in their efforts to increase sales and profitability. More importantly, SBI uses one-year and long-range strategic planning to help carry out its mission. A myriad of management-assistance seminars, informational workshops, minority-issue seminars, international marketing and sales workshops, and business strategy seminars are provided by SBI. Once a year it sponsors an information and technology conference for its members. SBI is supported by its business, professional, and industrial member firms as well as by government grants.

Mission Statement

The mission of SBI is to advance the commercial well-being of Raleigh-area small businesses by providing for economic expansion and serving the needs of member firms.

The Raleigh location employs eight professionals, including the director, the administrative assistant, the program development manager, two technical assistants, an accountant, an office specialist, and a receptionist. It has a business membership of 678. A council that represents a broad cross-section of membership governs the organization. It sets policies, establishes the budget, and oversees the work of the committees and task forces. The director is responsible for managing the professional staff. The staff at SBI includes:

Elijah J. Roberts, Director

Janelle Rainey, Program Development Manager

Melinda Chevez, Administrative Assistant

Your Name, Office Specialist

Cornell Fiazza, Receptionist

J. Elliott White, Technical Assistant, Service Businesses

Susan O'Hagen, Accountant

Enrique Ohmori, Technical Assistant, Product Businesses

An organization chart appears on page viii.

THE OFFICE SPECIALIST

You will be working as an office specialist for the director of the Small Business Institute (SBI) in Raleigh, North Carolina. As the office specialist, you will be responsible for preparing all word processing documents required by SBI.

Your major responsibility will be to assist with preparations for the upcoming annual conference and exposition sponsored by SBI. It will be held on May 8 and 9 at the Raleigh Suites and Convention Center. The theme of the conference is "E-Commerce and the New Economy." You will also be responsible for other word processing activities requested by other employees.

You will incorporate and reinforce your academic skills and develop an entrepreneurial spirit. More specifically, you will solve math problems using formulas; compose business correspondence; analyze, evaluate, synthesize, and organize information from a variety of sources; and gain a basic understanding of several entrepreneurial concepts.

Limited directions for completing the documents are provided. Therefore, you will need to examine each document closely, read the directions carefully, and use all available resources to process the documents.

Performance Tasks

- Process reports and manuscripts of moderate complexity.
- Establish and maintain computer files, and generate documents from stored data by inserting variables and manipulating text.
- Manipulate computer databases to store, retrieve, compile, or analyze information using Microsoft® Word for Windows®.
- Establish and maintain an office-filing system.
- Assist in routine personnel and financial transactions, keep non-complex personnel and fiscal records, and make routine purchases.
- Prepare and send correspondence and form letters.
- Compose documents.
- Edit and proofread materials for correct spelling and grammar as well as for format.
- Prepare confidential material and ensure that all information is kept confidential.

Knowledge, Skills, and Abilities

You will demonstrate the ability to interpret and follow oral and written rules and regulations; to function under difficult and high-pressure conditions; to maintain harmonious working relationships; to learn new practices, procedures, and equipment operations; to collect, assemble, and process information; and to organize work and make independent word processing decisions.

GENERAL DIRECTIONS

Read the guidelines below before you begin. Set up your folders as directed and then begin Job 1.

Reference Manual

Review the Reference Manual located in the back of this book before beginning. Most businesses adopt a standardized format to promote corporate identity and to improve productivity. SBI follows this commonly accepted practice.

Correspondence

A company letterhead template is stored on the data CD-ROM for use in preparing letters and memos. Save this letterhead as a document file using the job number. Prepare an envelope for each letter unless your instructor gives you other directions.

A company logo has also been provided; use it to "dress-up" documents such as newsletters or news releases.

Time-Saving Tips

Use automated features to move within documents, to search and replace text, to verify and clear formatting, or to copy styles or formatting.

Insert page numbers on multi-page documents. Insert a second page heading on two-page letters or memos.

Data CD

To complete your assignments, you will use the data CD-ROM in the back of this text or obtain those files from your instructor. To access the files from the data CD, follow the instructions on the CD label. Simply open the files when you are ready to use them.

File Management

Store your solutions to the jobs in a well-defined file management system. You will be doing most of your work for the administrative assistant, Melinda Chevez. Set up a folder for each person for whom you do work and save the jobs in the appropriate folders.

Proofreading and Preparing Documents for Distribution

You are a working professional, and as a professional, your documents must be error free. Establish a mindset that each document contains errors, and that you will find them. Before submitting documents to your employer (instructor), follow these steps.

1. Read each job carefully before beginning to key it. Consult the Reference Manual and other available resources to obtain the information you need to complete the assignment. Remember:

   • The Reference Manual provides you with sample formats for various documents.
   • Hints provide additional instructions for completing the documents.
   • An icon alerts you to files stored on your data CD that you will need to retrieve in order to complete the jobs.

2. Create a folder for each person on the staff and a miscellaneous folder. Check with your instructor to determine where you should create these folders.

3. Save each job in the appropriate folder using the job number as the file name; for example, Job 01, Job 02, etc. Save each file in the appropriate folders as directed previously.

4. Proofread all documents to be sure they are error free:

   • Use the Spelling and Grammar checks.
   • Proofread on screen and correct errors not detected by the software; use the thesaurus to enhance text.
   • Check placement and overall appearance before you print.
   • Check the printed document with the source copy.
   • Print and assemble documents appropriately for final distribution.

5. After completing each job, record the job number and date of completion in the Job Log in the Reference Manual section. When you receive your graded jobs from your instructor, record the grade in the appropriate space in the Job Log.

SBI ORGANIZATION CHART

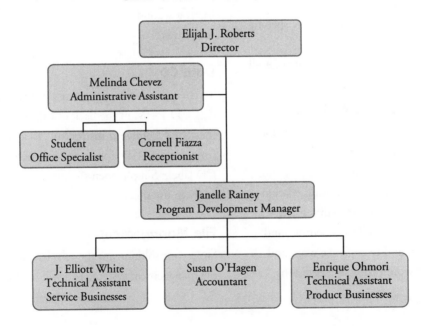

Jobs

S·B·I
SMALL BUSINESS INSTITUTE

FROM THE DESK OF MELINDA CHEVEZ, *Administrative Assistant*

January 6, 200-

Please retrieve the file Seminar Topics and make the changes indicated on the attached copy. Sort the list in alphabetical order by topics, but leave the pre-conference workshops at the end. After you sort, delete any extra space between topics or after the title. Modify the character spacing in the title to 200 percent. Then, position the workshop descriptions on the line below the workshop titles (delete the extra spaces). Be sure that all headings are formatted the same. Change the side margins to 1", and fit the document on one page.

hint:

Use the Shrink to Fit command in Print Preview to fit the job on one page.

2714 SPRING FOREST ROAD • RALEIGH, NC 27610-1997 • (919) 555-0126

Seminar Topics

FEATURES: Character Spacing
Format Painter
Margins
Shrink to Fit
Sort

SEMINAR TOPICS

Customer Satisfaction Program/Handling Customer Complaints A satisfied customer is a profitable customer. Learn to analyze your firm, identify customer needs, and maximize customer satisfaction. A satisfied customer is your most effective salesperson. The most effective ways to eliminate customer complaints and turn complaining customers into satisfied ones will be discussed.

E-Commerce and the New Economy The Internet has had a profound effect on the way we do business. Businesses are not limited by time and space anymore. Because of this, the "middle man" is not necessary. Businesses of all sizes are now able to conduct business and exchange information over the Internet. This workshop will focus on specific advantages and disadvantages of E-Commerce and E-Commerce models.

Traditional vs. Electronic Payment Methods This workshop will identify traditional and electronic payment methods used by businesses. Presentation will include security procedures for electronic payments.

Introduction to Export Marketing The purpose of this workshop is to acquaint interested persons with export sales, planning, financing, and documentation. In addition, sources of state and federal assistance in exporting will also be discussed.

Keeping a Successful Attitude This workshop provides Definite skills and techniques to overcome the negativism that bombards you daily. This is Not just a pump-up session. A systematic approach towards maintaining a positive attitude in your personal and professional life will be discussed

Defining Security Issues Any business, regardless of size, type, age, or any description, needs to be concerned about security; especially security of information and electronic networks. This workshop will identify various security issues and provide information for designing a security plan to protect your e-business.

Bidding and Quoting on Government Small Purchases Private sector insights on bidding and quoting on small purchases will be explored~~,~~ ~~along with~~ a representative from the Navy ^will^ explain~~ing~~ small purchase procedures.

Techniques for Collecting Accounts Receivable The topics include Proven Telephone Collection Techniques, Effective Collection Strategies, Specific Skills for Successful Negotiating, Special Arrangements to Guarantee Payment, Maximizing the Impact of Collect~~ing~~ ^on^ Letters, and Using Collection Laws to Your Advantage.

Planning and Budgeting--How to Survive in Business Effective planning and budgeting are ~~very~~ vital aspects of a successful business. Learn strategies that ~~you~~ empower you to insure the success of you^r^ business.

Developing an E-Business Plan for the Small Business The workshop will focus on developing a business plan to be used to seek funding as well serve as a blue^~~ ~~^print for your business. Learn the components of an effective plan for an e-business.

Pre-Conference Workshops

The ~~Basics of Being~~ ^ABCs of Becoming^ a Virtual Assistant ~~(VA)~~ ~~Getting~~ ^Becoming^ Certified

S·B·I
SMALL BUSINESS INSTITUTE

FROM THE DESK OF JANELLE RAINEY, PROGRAM DEVELOPMENT MANAGER

January 6, 200—

I have corrupted my Internet Marketing Workshop file. Please use the attached hard copy to create another flyer. Use your judgment to determine font size and styles, clip art, horizontal lines, text boxes, page borders, etc. However, please "bring to front" the name of the workshop on top of the selected clip art. Arrange all information attractively on the page.

This document should be saved in your portfolio. Refer to p. v for more information.

2714 SPRING FOREST ROAD • RALEIGH, NC 27610-1997 • (919) 555-0126

FEATURES: Borders and Shading
Clip Art
Font Types and Sizes
Lines
Object Order
Text Boxes
WordArt

The Small Business Institute

Presents

a workshop on

Internet Marketing

**Wednesday, May 8, 3:30 p.m.–4:45 p.m. and
Friday, May 10, 10:30 a.m.–11:45 a.m.**

at

Raleigh Suites and Convention Center

S·B·I
SMALL BUSINESS INSTITUTE

FROM THE DESK OF MELINDA CHEVEZ, ADMINISTRATIVE ASSISTANT

January 6, 200-

Use the attached business cards to create a data source file for the speakers who will be participating in the "E-Commerce and the New Economy" Conference and Exposition. Set this up in landscape to fit the data and use 1" margins. Sort the names into alphabetical order by last name.

Use the following fields:
title
firstname
lastname
company
address
city
state
ZIP
e-mail
phone
fax

MC

hint:

Do not include the header row in the sort.

2714 SPRING FOREST ROAD • RALEIGH, NC 27610-1997 • (919) 555-0126

FEATURES: Sort
Table

Attorney Darlene Johnson **Johnson Financial Services** 143 Chatham Road Raleigh, NC 27609-1786 Email: johnsond@jfs.com Phone: (919) 555-0101 Fax: (919) 555-0102	**Mr. Clarence Griffin** **Griffin Enterprises** 3256 Red Duck Court Durham, NC 27701-3781 Email: c_griffin@ge.net Phone: (919) 555-0190 Fax: (919) 555-0191
Dr. Vivian Hausler **Tri-Cities Chamber of Commerce** 857 Spence Circle Durham, NC 27705-3384 Email: vhausler@tccc.com Phone: (919) 555-0171 Fax: (919) 555-0172	**Mr. Carlos Hernandez** **Raleigh Community College** 716 Longdale Crescent Raleigh, NC 27608-1894 Email: chernandez@rcc.edu Phone: (919) 555-0185 Fax: (919) 555-0186
Ms. Donna Sawyer **Telenet Services, Inc.** 1405 New Charles Street Raleigh, NC 27604-1999 Email: dmsawyer@ts.org Phone: (919) 555-0158 Fax: (919) 555-0159	**Mr. Clyde O'Brien** **3629 Orchard Grove** Canton, NC 28716-3300 Email: cobrien@home.net Phone: (252) 555-0145 Fax: (252) 555-0144
Mrs. Williamena Octaviano **E-Commerce Solutions** 952 Spence Boulevard Durham, NC 27705-3384 Email: wictaviano@ecs.com Phone: (919) 555-0110 Fax: (919) 555-0120	**Miss Gwendolyn Srisvistan** **E-Assist, Inc.** 7433 Dehlman Way Charlotte, NC 28226-4303 Email: srisvistan_g@esi.net Phone: (704) 555-0111 Fax: (704) 555-0122
Ms. Roberta Sanchez **Sanchez Financial Services** 2345 Dunaway Drive Raleigh, NC 27608-1894 Email: sanchez@finser.com Phone: (919) 555-0167 Fax: (919) 555-0169	**Mr. Ben Suggs** **Suggs Technology** 192 Chestnut Road Raleigh, NC 27608-1895 Email: suggs@technology.com Phone: (919) 555-0154 Fax: (919) 555-0155

1/6/200-

Select a memo template and edit it
to include the SBI logo. Save the
memo template as SBI Memo.

Create an AutoText entry for the
name of the conference: "E-
Commerce and the New Economy"
Conference and Exposition. The conference name will appear in many of
the documents you will be working
on.

                    MC

hint:

*Save the macros and
template to your data
CD and not to the
hard drive or template
directory.*

Create macros for the closing lines of Elijah's and Melinda's
letters. Save the macros with the individuals' last names.
For Elijah's signature block, use the following information.
Be sure to add your reference initials to both macros.

    Sincerely

    Elijah J. Roberts, Director

For Melinda's signature block, use the following information.

    Sincerely

    Melinda Chevez
    Administrative Assistant

FEATURES: AutoText
Edit Template
Macro
Save As

Just the Fax

TO: Office Specialist

FAX: (919) 555-0127

FROM: Melinda Chevez

RE: Conference Registration Form

DATE: January 7, 200-

PAGES: 3, including this one

I am sending you a rough draft of the registration form. I
took it with me to my meeting and had time to fill in the rest
of the program. Please retrieve the Conference Registration
file and complete the brochure. If you have questions, I will
be in early tomorrow.

Melinda

Conference Registration

FEATURES: Cut and Paste
Graphic

PARTICIPANTS

add the participants' names and company names from Job 3. Center horizontally.

"E-COMMERCE AND THE NEW ECONOMY"
Conference and Expo

add appropriate graphic here

Presented by

SBI
Small Business Institute

May 8 and 9, 200-

To register for this exciting conference and expo, complete and detach the registration form below and mail with your payment to:

SBI
2714 Spring Forest Road
Raleigh, NC 27610-1997

- -

"E-COMMERCE AND THE NEW ECONOMY"
CONFERENCE & EXPO *spell out*

REGISTRATION FORM

Company Name _____ Phone _____
Address _____ ZIP _____
Name and Title _____
Registrations _____ @ $99 = $ _____
           _____ @ $79 = $ _____ (for 2 or more persons
                                       from same company)
           Total enclosed $ _____
_____ Check made payable to SBI _____ Purchase Order # _____

SBI
Small Business Institute

proudly presents

"E-Commerce and the New Economy" Conference and Expo

Plan to join us and learn how you can make your small business survive and thrive. Below is a list of workshops that will be presented.

E-Commerce and the New Economy
Traditional vs. Electronic Payment Methods
Bidding and Quoting on Government Small Purchases
Customer Satisfaction Program/Handling Customer Complaints
Developing an E-Business Plan for the Small Business
Keeping a Successful Attitude
Planning and Budgeting--How to Survive in Business
Protecting Your Personnel Investment
Techniques for Collecting Accounts Receivable
Defining Security Issues

BONUS PRE-CONFERENCE WORKSHOPS

ABCs of Becoming
The Basics of Being a Virtual Assistant (VA)
Getting Certified
Becoming

HOTEL ACCOMMODATIONS

A special rate of $75 per night has been secured for participants attending the conference here at the Raleigh Suites and Convention Center. If you would like to reserve a room, call the hotel directly at 1-800-555-1999.
010

use color

PROGRAM

Thursday, May 8

8:00 a.m.-12:00 noon	Registration
9:00 a.m.-11:30 a.m.	Pre-Conference Workshops / *The ABCs of Becoming a Virtual Assistant* / *Becoming Certified*
12 noon-1:00 p.m.	Opening Session and Luncheon / Ms. Roberta Sanchez, Speaker / President, Sanchez Financial Services
2:00 p.m.-3:15 p.m.	Concurrent Sessions
3:30 p.m.-4:45 p.m.	Concurrent Sessions
5:30 p.m.-6:30 p.m.	Business Networking and Card Exchange
6:30 p.m.-8:30 p.m.	Banquet / Mr. Ben Suggs, Speaker / Chairman & CEO, Suggs Technology Corp.

Friday, May 9

7:30 a.m.-8:30 a.m.	*Continental Breakfast*
8:45 a.m.-10:00 a.m.	*Concurrent Sessions*
10:15 a.m.-11:30 a.m.	*Concurrent Sessions*
11:30 a.m.-12:00 noon	*Checkout*
12:15 p.m.-1:30 p.m.	*Closing Sessions and Luncheon*

From: Melinda Chevez [mchevez@sbi.org]
To: Office Specialist [ospecialist@sbi.org]
Date: January 8, 200-   10:22 AM
Subject: Conference Participants

Please retrieve last year's conference participants from the Access data file, Contacts (insert it into Word). Sort the table by company in ascending order, then by city. Choose a Table AutoFormat for the table and adjust the column widths so the table looks attractive. Save the file as Job 06a.

Add the eight additional participants from the copy of my contact list. Delete the records Kanawha Medical Supply, Inc. and Watson, Incorporated. They have gone out of business. Sort the list in ascending order by company and city again. Print one copy of the file. Save the file as Job 06b.

Compare the two documents (without formatting) and merge them into a new document. Save the file as Job 06c.

Contacts

hint:

Display the Database toolbar in Word (View, Toolbars, Database) to insert the database into a Word document. Use the toolbar buttons to sort and to add and delete records. Change the page orientation to landscape, and repeat the headings on each page of the table.

FEATURES: Add Records
Adjust Column Widths
Compare Documents
Delete Records
Heading Rows Repeat
Sort
Table AutoFormat

Davis, Cindy

Full Name:	Ms. Cindy Davis
Company:	Telenet Services
Business:	7865 Fourth Street
	Raleigh, NC 27607-1254

Johnson, Barbara

Full Name:	Mrs. Barbara Johnson
Company:	City of Raleigh
Business:	1120 S. City Hall Avenue
	Raleigh, NC 27709-3362

Davenport, James

Full Name:	Mr. James Davenport
Company:	Walker Enterprises
Business:	9402 Randsell Circle
	Raleigh, NC 27615-1320

Banks, Susan

Full Name:	Ms. Susan Banks
Company:	Morgan Lawn Care
Business:	3301 Thomas Street
	Raleigh, NC 27605-1876

Lopez, Christine

Full Name:	Ms. Christine Lopez
Company:	Laverne's Florist
Business:	703 Thimble Road
	Raleigh, NC 27610-1122

Mendez, Rosa

Full Name:	Miss Rosa Mendez
Company:	Good Books, Inc.
Business:	675 Mt. Pleasant Road
	Raleigh, NC 27608-1656

Ortiz, Hector

Full Name:	Mr. Hector Ortiz
Company:	Invisions Optometrist
Business:	987 Deep Creek Boulevard
	Raleigh, NC 27607-1465

White, Louis

Full Name:	Mr. Louis White
Company:	Internet Resources Group
Business:	857 Spence Circle
	Raleigh, NC 27611-1233

S·B·I
SMALL BUSINESS INSTITUTE

FROM THE DESK OF MELINDA CHEVEZ, *ADMINISTRATIVE ASSISTANT*

January 9, 200-

Please prepare the attached letter for Elijah's signature. Merge with the source file you created in Job 3. Also prepare a set of mailing labels. Print only the first letter and the set of labels. Save the form letter as Job 07a, the merged letters as Job 07b, and the merged labels as Job 07c.

MC

hint:

Remember to use the macro for closing lines.

2714 SPRING FOREST ROAD • RALEIGH, NC 27610-1997 • (919) 555-0126

FEATURES: Labels
Macro
Mail Merge

(Insert title and last name), thank you so very much for agreeing to serve as a workshop speaker for our "E-Commerce and the New Economy" Conference and Exposition, which will be held on May 8 and 9 at Raleigh Suites and Convention Center.

The presentations and workshops of this year's conference are designed to keep the small business owner informed of not only the essential tools for keeping the business afloat but also the latest technological trends in the industry.

We are looking forward to a great conference, and your participation will assist us in making this the best conference ever. If you need additional information, please call (919) 555-0126, or send an e-mail message to eroberts@sbi.org.

S·B·I
SMALL BUSINESS INSTITUTE

FROM THE DESK OF MELINDA CHEVEZ, ADMINISTRATIVE ASSISTANT

1/9/200-

Please prepare our SBI Publications list as a 1-page form that can be completed in Word, and then e-mailed or faxed. Insert SBI Publications as a diagonal text watermark. Use 1" margins and set it up as a table. Make the changes indicated on the attached copy.

hint:
Adjust the watermark so that it does not interfere with reading the text. Also, protect the document.

2714 SPRING FOREST ROAD • RALEIGH, NC 27610-1997 • (919) 555-0126

FEATURES: Borders and Shading
Forms Toolbar
Protect Document
Shrink to Fit
Table
Watermark

sbi publications	PRICE

☐ ***Basics of E-Concepts. A Beginner's Guide to Starting an Online Business.*** A practical guide that provides a detailed glossary of concepts and outlines step-by-step the most successful methods for starting an e-commerce business.
120 pages   s/n 044-078-003251-8 $10.95

add a line between items

☐ ***Getting Your E-Business Off the Ground.*** This publication identifies the top ten emerging strategies that will make any business leading edge in the 21st Century. It also covers the changes in marketing strategies brought about by the Internet.
155 pages   s/n 044-099-003217-9 $14.99

☐ ***So You Want To Start an E-Business: The Pros and Cons of Electronic Payments*** For electronic payments, security is the key. This booklet provides an overview of the techniques, payment systems, and security guidelines used to enable payments to be made over the internet.
60 pages   s/n 044-023-102682-10 $7.25

☐ **Launching Your E-Business.** This is a blueprint to help executives understand e-commerce objectives and how to plan a Web site by outlining the strategies for implementing a business over the Internet beforehand. *use the same font throughout*
128 pages   s/n 044-123-71982-11 $12.95

☐ ***Starting and Managing a Small Business.*** The dream of creating and leading a successful enterprise depends upon the practical aspects of such a venture, including the risks. These are discussed in this Starting and Managing series book.
160 pages   s/N 044-098-003217-12 $18.~~25~~ 00

☐ ***A Handbook on Small Business*** Finance This book provides a starting point for small business ~~individuals~~ owners or managers who want to sharpen their financial management skills.
158 pages   s/n 044-123-456780-13 $12.85

DO NOT DETACH - RETURN ENTIRE FORM

Enclosed is ☐ checks _____   ☐ Credit card _____
line up ☐ money order _____   ☐ Purchase order _____
the boxes   ☐ On account _____

Send to: Small Business Institute   **Telephone:**   (919) 555-0126
          2714 Spring Forest Road   **Fax:**   (919) 555-0127
          Raleigh, NC 27610-1977   **E-mail:**   publications@sbi.org

Name: _____

Street Address: _____

City: _____   **State:** ☐   **ZIP Code:** _____

DO NOT DETACH - RETURN ENTIRE FORM

January 10, 200-

Please key the attached summer schedule. It will be sent to the members of SBI. You may include the SBI logo. Fit the table to the contents.   MC

SBI

*(add the address,
phone number, and e-mail address)*

Summer Class Schedule

Date	Days	Course Title	Time	Room	Cost
June 2 & 4	M W	MS Project	7-9 p.m.	C21	$50
June 3 & 5	T R	MS Project	7-9 p.m.	C21	$50
June 9, 11, 16, 18	M W	Windows XP	7-9 p.m.	C23	$100
June 10, 12, 17, 19	T R	MS Word	7-9 p.m.	C23	$100
June 16, 18, 23, 25	M W	Acrobat Writer	7-9 p.m.	C20	$125
June 21 & 28	S	MS Access	9-11 a.m.	C22	$100
July 7, 9, 14, 16	M W	MS PowerPoint	7-9 p.m.	C21	$100
July 8, 10, 15, 17	T R	Dream Weaver	7-9 p.m.	C22	$125
July 19 & 26	S	MS Excel	8 a.m.-4 p.m.	C21	$50
July 21, 23, 28, 30	M W	Flash	7-9 p.m.	C22	$125
August 5 & 6	M W	Word 2003 Review	8 a.m.-12 p.m.	B6	$75
August 12 & 14	M W	MS Publisher	8 a.m.-12 p.m.	B6	$50
August 20 & 22	T R	Photo Shop	9-11 a.m.	B6	$75
August 27 & 29	T R	IC3 Review	8 a.m.-12 p.m.	B6	$75

To Register: Call SBI at 919-555-0126 or e-mail ospecialist@sbi.org. You will be given directions for registering for any of the above courses. Class size is limited, so register early.

M = Monday, T = Tuesday, W = Wednesday, R = Thursday, F = Friday, S = Saturday (fit this all on one line)

hint:

Set this up as a table and use AutoFit to Contents.

FEATURES: AutoFit to Contents
Table

S·B·I
SMALL BUSINESS INSTITUTE

FROM THE DESK OF SUSAN O'HAGEN, ACCOUNTANT

January 10, 200–

Please retrieve the Course Revenue data file and complete the form using the attached information. (Revenue = Enrollment x Cost per Student.) Use 10 percent shading in the title row, a double outside border, and format the rest of the table according to our reference manual.

hint:

If you are familiar with Excel, you may want to set this up as a spreadsheet.

2714 SPRING FOREST ROAD • RALEIGH, NC 27610-1997 • (919) 555-0126

Course Revenue

FEATURES: Borders and Shading
Formulas
Tables

SMALL BUSINESS INSTITUTE

Summary of Computer Courses Offered

Fourth
~~Third~~ Quarter

	Course Title	Sessions	Enrollment	Cost Per Student	Revenue
1.	Corel WordPerfect 8	3	57	50	
2.	Corel WordPerfect 11	2	23	50	
3.	MicroSoft Windows ~~98~~ XP	7	111	50	
4.	MicroSoft Windows 2000	6	97	50	
5.	MicroSoft Word 2003	3	47	50	
6.	MicroSoft Excel 2003	4	47	50	
7.	MicroSoft Access 2003	6	101	75	
8.	MicroSoft PowerPoint 2003	4	58	50	
9.	MicroSoft Outlook 2003	3	33	50	
10.	Quicken	2	19	75	
11.	Quattro Pro	2	71	75	
12.	Desktop Publishing	4	27	50	
13.	MicroSoft Publisher	2	24	50	
14.	MicroSoft Project Manager	3	48	75	
	Totals				

use the formula to determine revenues

Total columns 2, 3, and 5.

S·B·I
SMALL BUSINESS INSTITUTE

FROM THE DESK OF MELINDA CHEVEZ, *ADMINISTRATIVE ASSISTANT*

January 9, 200-

One of the presenters faxed information he plans to use for his session and asked that we prepare a handout for him.

Please key this in report format, making all of the indicated changes. Key the source line as a footnote that follows the subtitle.

MC

2714 SPRING FOREST ROAD • RALEIGH, NC 27610-1997 • (919) 555-0126

FEATURES: Bullets and
Numbering
Footnote
Justification
Margins

Justify the paragraphs

WILL THAT BE CASH, CHECK, OR CHARGE?) *14pt. bold all caps*

TYPES OF ELECTRONIC PAYMENT[1]) *12pt. bold caps and lc*

One of the major differences between conducting business traditionally and conducting business electronically, is the way in which payment is received. Traditionally, cash, checks, credit cards, and most recently, debit cards, have been used to pay for goods and services.

When business is conducted online, payment is also made online. This type of payment is referred to as an electronic payment. It is transmitted either over telephone lines or between Web sites on the Internet. All information is in digital form only. The following payment options are the most used in the e-commerce industry.

- E-Checks   *add a fancy bullet to each head.*

indent 0.5" on both sides] An **e-check** is an encrypted representation of a paper check. The customer fills in the check online then sends it via a secure server to the recipient. The amount specified on the e-check is electronically withdrawn from the sender's account and then deposited into the recipient's account.

- E-Cash

E-cash is also referred to as ***Scrip, digital cash***, or ***digital coins***. A customer can buy e-cash and store it in a digital wallet on the hard drive. The digital wallet is electronically linked to the customer's bank account and can be refilled at any time. Payments made with e-cash are preauthorized and anonymous. E-cash is often used to pay for electronic goods purchased over the Internet such as software.

- Smart Cards

A **smart card** is usually the size of a credit card and has an electronic memory built in. Smart cards are used to store such things as medical information, insurance information, and even electronic cash.

- Electronic Wallets

E-wallets are sometimes referred to as ***digital wallets***. An e-wallet is a software program that contains a person's information that is needed for making electronic payments. This information, including credit card numbers, bank account information, and contact information, is encrypted so that security is ensured.

[1] Source: *E-Commerce Concepts*, Carol M. Cram, Course Technology/Thomson Learning, Boston, MA, 2001.

S·B·I
SMALL BUSINESS INSTITUTE

FROM THE DESK OF MELINDA CHEVEZ, ADMINISTRATIVE ASSISTANT

January 9, 200-

Please use the attached information to create an attractive flyer to announce the upcoming e-commerce conference. Use WordArt, color, fonts, and other good design principles to make this flyer "pop." We plan to post this on our Web site later, so insert a hyperlink to the document you prepared in Job 1 where it says to click on seminar topics. That way, visitors to our site can "jump" to the list of topics.

Save the file as a Word document (Job 12a) and also as a Web page (Job 12b).

2714 SPRING FOREST ROAD • RALEIGH, NC 2~

S B I

presents an

E-Commerce Conference

May 8 & 9, 200-

**Raleigh Suites and Convention Center
Raleigh, North Carolina**

Registration Fee: $149.00

This conference is designed to present and illustrate information regarding using the Internet to conduct business. It is for anyone interested in learning more about doing business online.

You will learn:

➢ how e-commerce works
➢ how to design and maintain an effective Web site
➢ how to avoid e-commerce mistakes

➢ how to attract and keep customers
➢ how to reduce traditional operating costs
➢ how to expand markets
➢ and so much more.

Click seminar topics to see a list of conference topics.

For further information, contact:

SBI

2714 Spring Forest Road
Raleigh, NC 27610-1997
Phone: (919) 555-0126
Fax: (919) 555-0217

or

www.sbi.org

FEATURES: Font Sizes and Styles
Hyperlink
Save as Web Page

SBI presents an

E-Commerce Conference

May ~~7~~ *8* & ~~8~~ *9*, 200-

Raleigh Suites and Convention Center

Raleigh, North Carolina

Registration Fee

~~Cost:~~ $149.00

This conference is designed to present and illustrate ~~what you need to know in order to use~~ *how to conduct business over* the Internet ~~to conduct business.~~ It is for anyone interested in learning more about doing business online.

You will learn how e-commerce works, how to attract and keep customers, how to design and maintain an effective Web site, how to avoid e-commerce mistakes, how to reduce traditional operating costs, how to expand markets, and so much more.

Click (seminar topics) to see a list of conference topics.
create a hyperlink

For further information, contact:

SBI

2714 Spring Forest Road

Raleigh, NC 27610-1997

Phone: (919) 555-0126

Fax: (919) 555-0217

or

www.sbi.org

S·B·I
SMALL BUSINESS INSTITUTE

FROM THE DESK OF ELIJAH J. ROBERTS, DIRECTOR

January 10, 200-

☐ Read	☐ Approve
☒ Handle	☐ Forward
☐ Correct	☐ Review with me

Create a reading bookmark that can be given as a souvenir at the "E-Commerce and the New Economy" Conference and Exposition. Please include the SBI logo. Use the attached information and mark-up. Use your judgment in choosing appropriate fonts and bullets. Bold the six paragraph headings.

Research at least eight Internet sources to add to the back of the bookmark. Put them in a bulleted list and be sure to include the Web addresses.

hint:

Use the Table feature with one column and one row or draw a text box to create the bookmark.

2714 SPRING FOREST ROAD • RALEIGH, NC 27610-1997

S·B·I
SMALL BUSINESS INSTITUTE

E-Commerce Tips for Small Businesses*

- **Offer Discounts and Specials.** Offer specials for your online customers only.

- **Send an Electronic Newsletter and Other Promotional Materials.** Build relationships with your customers. Maintain their names and addresses in an electronic database. Keep customers and potential customers up to date with new products or trends in your industry. Keep the newsletter interesting.

- **Keep Current on Latest Trends.** Check out other e-commerce Web sites. Study your competition.

- **Use Banner Exchange.** Banner Exchange will give you the needed visibility to generate sales.

- **Subscribe to Search Engines.** Allow your company to be reached by a greater audience.

- **Keep Your Web Site Up to Date.** Don't keep out-of-date information on your Web site.

Source: *Score Business Advice. www.score.org

Move your business into the new millennium with e-commerce

Important Internet Resources:

- Electronic Commerce Guide www.ecommerce.internet.com

- Microsoft bCentral Commerce Manager www.bcentral.com

- United States Small Business Administration www.sba.gov

- Issues in Small Business www.mssb.com

- Buy E-Commerce Basics www.amazon.com

- Dan Keller's E-Commerce Basics www.keller.com/ecomm

- E-Commerce Times www.ecommerce.times.com

- Interworld www.interworld.com

SBI
2714 Spring Forest Road
Raleigh, NC 27610-1997

Phone: (919) 555-0126
Web Address: www.sbi.org
Fax: (919) 555-0127

FEATURES: Borders and Shading
Bullets and Numbering
Clip Art
Internet Research
Tables
Text Boxes

E-Commerce Tips for Small Businesses*

- Offer Discounts and Specials. Offer specials for your online customers only.

- Send an Electronic Newsletter and Other Promotional Materials. Build relationships with your customers. Maintain their names and addresses in an electronic database. Keep customers and potential customers up to date with new products or trends in your industry. Keep the newsletter interesting.

- Keep Current on Latest Trends. Check out other e-commerce Web sites. Study your competition.

  Use Banner Exchange. Banner Exchange will give you the needed visibility to generate sales.

- Subscribe to Search Engines. Allow your company to be reached by a greater audience.

- Keep Your Web Site Up to Date. Don't keep out-of-date information on your Web site.

Source: *Score Business Advice: www.score.org

Motto: Move your business into the new millennium with E-Commerce!

Please use the mark-up on following page to arrange the information.

The bookmark will be 8" long x 2.5" wide.

Front

Back

SBJ Logo

Graphic Image

E-Commerce Tips for
Small Businesses

Motto

Important Internet
Resources:

Use fancy bullets.

Add source line

Company Name and
Address

S·B·I
SMALL BUSINESS INSTITUTE

FROM THE DESK OF ELIJAH J. ROBERTS, *DIRECTOR*

January 10, 200-

☐ Read	☐ Approve
☒ Handle	☐ Forward
☐ Correct	☐ Review with me

hint:

Use the Roman numeral outline feature. Remember to capitalize each section appropriately.

Please key the attached outline. Send a copy to Dr. Barbara M. Willis, E-Personal Assistant, 288 Thomas Paine Drive, Virginia Beach, VA 23464-1999, for her review and approval. This is the outline that Dr. Willis and I will use to prepare our PowerPoint presentation for the National Business Virtual Assistant Conference.

Please draft a cover letter and provide an envelope. Please sign the letter for me.

2714 SPRING FOREST ROAD • RALEIGH, NC 27610-1997 • (919) 555-0126

FEATURES: Bullets and Numbering
Envelopes and Labels
Macro

Electronic Commerce

①   Introduction

^②   Electronic Commerce Terminology

③ ②   Effective E-Commerce Strategies

④   a. Develop ~~your~~ ^{a great} product

        b. Build ~~the~~ ^a site that sells

        c. Attract targeted customers

④   Electronic payment methods

        a. credit cards

        b. smart cards

        c. electronic check

        d. micropayments

⑤   Advertising ~~over the internet~~ ^{stet}

7 ⑥   Security issues   insert

⑧   Search engines and directory

⑨   Conclusions   ⑥   Purchasing over the Internet

⑩   Q & A   ⓐ email

                                      ⓑ order form

                                      ⓒ electronic cart

SMALL BUSINESS INSTITUTE

FROM THE DESK OF MELINDA CHEVEZ, *ADMINISTRATIVE ASSISTANT*

January 15, 200-

We need to put our teaching contract on line. Key the teaching contract that is attached, making the indicated corrections. You will use it later to prepare individual contracts.

Create this as a table, add borders between the sections, insert the appropriate fields, and protect the form. Rotate and center the text in cells as shown. Add 5% shading to the cells with rotated text. Add 5% shading to the row with the course names. Add fields as necessary to fill in the form. Set the length for State to 2, and format the text for uppercase.

Protect and save the form. Test the form.

MC

hint:

Protect the document as a form.

2714 SPRING FOREST ROAD • RALEIGH, NC 27610-1997 • (919) 555-0126

FEATURES: Borders and Shading
Forms Toolbar
Merge and Split Cells
Protect Form
Rotate Text
Table

Add the SBI logo at the center. Center and key the form title in small caps.

Teaching Contract

Personal Data

Shade →

Name:	Date:
Address:	
City:	State: Zip:
No. of Courses:	Term:
Social Security No.:	

Employment Conditions

Insert the copy below as the first paragraph.

Acceptance of this contract includes acceptance of the general conditions of employment set forth in the policy manual of the Small Business Institute. Incompetence, inadequate or unsatisfactory performance of duties, insubordination, or misconduct are grounds for immediate removal.

If the terms of this appointment are acceptable to you, please sign, date, and return the original and one copy of this contract to the administrative office. You will **NOT** be placed on the payroll until the signed contract has been returned.

Special Conditions:

Course Title

5% Shading

Course Title	Course Code	Lecture Hours	Lab Hours	Total Credit Hours

---

Rate Per Credit Hour	$	x Credit Hours:	= Total Gross Salary:	$

Payroll Use Only

Shade →

Log Number:	P/R Pay Period:	Check No.:
Voucher No.:	P/R Number:	Check Date:
Comments:		

The Institute reserves the right to cancel any class prior to the time that the class next meets following the drop/add session in which the class begins. There are no provisions for payment for partial services in the event the class is canceled. The contract period starts the first day of class and ends the last day of class.

From: Enrique Ohmori [eohmori@sbi.org]
To: Office Specialist [ospecialist@sbi.org]
Date: January 16, 200- 9:28 AM
Subject: SBI Directory

 Sketch

We want to prepare a member directory that is 5.5" by 8.5". See the attached sketch for a possible format. Change the paper size to 5.5" x 8.5" and the side margins to 0.5". Insert a 2-column, 3-row table. Insert the fields in column 1, adjust the rows to a height of 2", make all font changes and such, then copy the information in the first cell to all the other cells. Use a larger sans serif font for the names, and a 10-pt. font for the rest of the information. Be sure to insert the field *NextRecord* after each member's information. Add a horizontal line to the header and footer and include the page numbers as *Page x of x* in the footer aligned at the right. Merge the names from the data file, SBI Members. Put the directory in alphabetical order by members' last names.

Be creative and design covers for the front and back pages. Please include an appropriate motto and the SBI address on the back.

Print the directory in landscape orientation and two documents per page. Save the directory as Job 16a and the covers as Job 16b.

SBI Members

FEATURES: Access Database
Borders and Shading
Clip Art
Custom Size
Form Fields
Mail Merge
Page Numbering
Page Setup
Print (2 pages per sheet)
Tables

Last Name, First Name	Last name, First Name
Company Name	Company Name
Street Address	Street Address
City, State ZIP	City, State ZIP
Phone:	**Phone:**
Fax:	**Fax:**
E-mail:	**E-mail:**

FRONT COVER   BACK COVER

SBI Logo

Directory of Members

Insert an
appropriate
graphic

Motto

SBI Address

From: Elijah J. Roberts [eroberts@sbi.org]
To: Office Specialist [ospecialist@sbi.org]
Date: January 16, 200-   4:15 PM
Subject: Expense Report

Please use the figures below to prepare my expense report for the regional meeting in Greenville.
Print two copies. Use the data file, Expense Report.

1/10   Registration - $150.00   1/12   Lodging - $121.29
       Travel - $378.90   Breakfast - $10.20
       Lodging - $121.29   Lunch - $16.86
       Lunch - $18.21

1/11   Lodging - $121.29   1/13   Breakfast - $9.89
       Breakfast - $10.21
       Dinner - $31.88

hint:

*Be sure to align the
numbers at the right.*

Expense Report

FEATURES: Formula
Justification
Table

January 17, 200-

Please key and format these "Virtual Assistant" handouts for the pre-conference workshops. Format them as DS reports. These handouts will also be posted on our Web site, so save them as html files. Choose a default Word style for the side headings, but whatever style you choose, be consistent throughout. Use the Title style for the title. Be sure to check spelling and grammar. I noticed a few errors in these materials.

Save the first handout as Job 18a and the second handout as Job 18b. Save the html files as Job 18c.

G. Elliot White

hint:

To see a complete list of available Word styles, press and hold the shift key as you click the down arrow to the right of the styles box on the toolbar.

Evaluation Matrix; VA Certification

FEATURES: Bullets and Numbering
Footnotes
Line Spacing
Save As
Styles

Handout #1: The ABCs of Becoming a Virtual Assistant

Introduction

You have worked in a support role for years and the idea of having your own business, using your talents, and doing work you love is appealing. You have heard about "virtual assistant," but you is not sure exactly what it is and what it involves; however, you believe that it is something worth investigating.

What Is a Virtual Assistant?

A virtual assistant is a independent entrepreneur providing administrative, creative, and/or technical services. Utilizing advanced technological modes of communication and data delivery, a professional virtual assistant assists clients in his or her area of expertise from their own office on a contractual basis.

In essence, a virtual assistant is a professional who works for a business but in his or her own office space.

How Can a Virtual Assistant Be Used?

- A large company may use a VA for any secreterial work that a full-time administrative assistant cannot handle—peak periods, major projects, etc.
- A small business with no regular staff may need assistance with desktop publishing, such as creating brochures, newsletters, flyers, and direct mail.

Types of Support

Virtual assistants provide

- Support to small businesses that have the potential to expand.
- Management and technical assistance, private and public sector referrals.
- One-on-one marketing.
- Financial and international counseling to existing and start-up business.
- Administrative and office support to any business or entrepreneur.
- Support to firms in there efforts to increase sales and profitability.

Example of Services

Virtual assistants can provide a wide variety of services, including

- Correspondence
- Mailing list maintenance
- Desktop publishing
- Announcements
- Brochures
- Business cards
- Flyers
- Invitations

- Newsletters
- Document/file conversion
- Editing and proofreading
- Basic Web design

Methods for Transferring Correspondence
A virtual assistant may use one or all of these methods to transfer correspondence or other project material to a client
- E-mail
- Fax
- Mail or courier services
- Express mail services

Advantages
There are many advantages to using a virtual assistant. Some of these advantages are
- The assistant is available 284 hours a day, 7 days a week, 365 days a year.
- Clients pay only for the time spent and materials used.
- There are no fringe benefits to pay. Clients eliminate
  - Medical, dental, and vision care benefited.
  - Payroll taxes.
  - Paid vacations.
  - Worker compensation ensurance.
  - Federal and state unemployment taxes.

Handout 2: Becoming Certified

Becoming certified as a virtual assistant may assist you in your ticket to a brighter future. Earning certification as a VA acknowledges your expertise in a given area. This certification will help businesses and clients recognize that your credentials are a cut above the rest. You have been certified that the skills and knowledge you've gained through experience are top-notch.

VA certification provides professionals with the necessary skills to maximize any company's investment. Increasingly, businesses are outsourcing more and more functions. Market your company effectively and earn a share of the outsource market.

There are two levels of certification[1]:

1. PVA (Professional Virtual Assistant) is the first of the two levels of certification. The PVA designation tells the world that you are a professional who has invested in your career through education, training, and actual hands-on experience. This designation also shows the public that your accomplishments have been independently evaluated and that you are near the top of your field.

2. MVA (Master Virtual Assistant) is the pinnacle of the certification program. This level consists of VAs who have expanded their education with additional courses pertaining to their practice and who have more depth of experience by taking on a variety of tasks and projects.

Becoming certified is not an easy task, but there are agencies willing to provide you with the tools and support to become certified.

How Do You Become Certified?
Submit an application to an independent credentialing authority. This authority will review your references, verify your work experience, and evaluate your education as if you were applying for a job.

What Are the Evaluation Criteria?

- Education
- Certifications
- Work experience
- References
- Computer skills

The following table shows the criteria and points approved by the Board of Directors of the Virtual Assistant Certification Association of America.

Insert the data file Evaluation Matrix here.

---

[1] www.vacertification.com

What Are the Advantages of Certification?

- Provides industry recognition of your knowledge and proficiency
- Shows that you are committed to your job
- Promotes self-confidence that comes from knowing you are a professional
- Is nationally recognized and sanctioned
- Reassures clients that you have met national standards and guidelines
- Increases personal credibility and marketability
- Increases professionalism

What Are the Potential Benefits?

- Discounts on products and services
- Subscription to the professional magazine
- Recognition through a Code of Conduct
- Information about upcoming trends in the industry
- Seminars and conferences
- Networking opportunities

What Are International Virtual Assistants?

Many virtual assistants from different countries are certified each year. The number of VAs certified this year has been broken down by country in the following chart.

Insert the chart from the Excel data file VA Certification here.

From: Melinda Chevez [mchevez@sbi.org]
To: Office Specialist [ospecialist@sbi.org]
Date: January 20, 200-   2:10 PM
Subject: Interview Schedule

Please open the data file, Interview Schedule, and make the following changes.

- Convert the text to a table.
- Center and bold the text in the header row.
- Shade the header row 15% gray and apply double lines around it.
- Increase the row height for all rows to 0.3".
- Center the text in header row vertically.

hint:

Select only the lines in the text; don't highlight blank lines.

Interview Schedule

FEATURES: Borders and Shading
Cell Alignment
Justification
Page Setup
Row Height
Table, Convert

S·B·I
SMALL BUSINESS INSTITUTE

FROM THE DESK OF ELIJAH J. ROBERTS, *Director*

January 20, 200-

I sent a draft of this letter to Melinda for her to review. She used Track Changes to make changes and made several comments. Please retrieve the Chase Letter file, read the comments and corrections she made, make any appropriate changes, and then delete the comments and accept or delete the changes. Be sure to add a second page header. Proofread carefully and use the grammar checker. Create an envelope.

2714 SPRING FOREST ROAD • RALEIGH, NC 27610-1997 • (919) 555-0126

Chase Letter

FEATURES: Comments
Header and Footer
Macro
Spelling and Grammar
Track Changes

S·B·I
SMALL BUSINESS INSTITUTE

FROM THE DESK OF MELINDA CHEVEZ, *ADMINISTRATIVE ASSISTANT*

January 20, 200-

Please prepare a post card invitation for the upcoming small breakfast forum on May 12 using Avery 5389. Make the front of the post card visually appealing. Split the cell on the back side and key the invitation text at the left in a fancy font and add a border around it. I've attached a sample layout. Add merge fields to the address section on the right; then merge the post cards with the presenters' data file you created in Job 3.

hint:

Create the document using the Label feature. Set up all text and graphics on the post card and make all necessary changes. Then display the Mail Merge toolbar and insert the Address field and the Next Record field before you complete the merge.

2714 SPRING FOREST ROAD • RALEIGH, NC 27610-1997 • (919) 555-0126

FEATURES: Borders
Clip Art
Envelopes and Labels
Fonts
Lines and Text Boxes
Mail Merge

Side 2

You are cordially invited to a
Small Business Breakfast Forum
On May 12, 200-
7:45 a.m. until 9:30 a.m.
in the Raleigh Suites and
Convention Center
1123 Fourth Street, Raleigh, NC

RSVP by April 1

Phone: (919) 555-0126
Fax: (919) 555-0127
E-mail: ospecialist@sbi.org

Add the SBI
logo here

Stamp

name and address here

Side 1

Please color the background.

Add
appropriate
clip art to
make this
appealing.

Insert the date and
shade the background.

Electronic Payment Solutions

From: Elijah J. Roberts [eroberts@sbi.org]
To: Office Specialist [ospecialist@sbi.org]
Date: January 20, 200-   1:15 PM
Subject: Working Draft

The data file Coaching Initiative is a working draft of a program initiative that SBI hopes to launch soon. Before implementation, our Board of Directors will need to approve. You'll find additional copy to be inserted in your in basket (see next page).

Format this as an unbound report. Please track all changes. Check for spelling and grammar errors. Create a title page and a table of contents, and number all pages. I am still working on the budget. Use styles for the primary headings in the table of contents to create a hyperlink to move quickly to each section. Insert the watermark DRAFT diagonally on all pages. Save this as Job 22a.

Please AutoSummarize the report for my meeting. You don't need to format the summary. I will use this draft as a "talking point" sheet for our meeting. Create this as a new document. Print a copy of the auto summary and save the report again as a different version, Job 22b.

Change the words *small business* and *small businesses* to *e-commerce business* and *e-commerce businesses* throughout. Carefully check any elements (such as *a/an* as needed after making these changes. Save this again as a different version, Job 22c.

hint:

Adjust the watermark so that it does not interfere with the reading of the text. Use a section break between the title page and table of contents.

Coaching Initiative

FEATURES: AutoSummarize
Borders and Shading
Change Case
Headers and Footers
Search and Replace
Spelling and Grammar
Styles
Table of Contents

Insert A

Athletes, performers, and politicians have long understood how this work. It is called working with a mentor or a coach. In simple terms, this using a talent and trained coach to assist you in achieving your goals and dreams. A coach or mentor can take you beyond what you ever thought possible. Teaming up with a coach creates a positive, can-do attitude that supports you in consistently moving forward. A mentor or coach can assist you in seeing beyond any limitations-you can see all those trees and bushes in the forest. Therefore, SBJ is seeking funds to begin a Coaching and Mentoring Network Initiative for Small Businesses.

Insert B

Expectations of Mentees
- Must be competitive.
- Must be committed.
- Must have a mindset to share information.
- Must have the need to establish milestones.

S·B·I
SMALL BUSINESS INSTITUTE

FROM THE DESK OF JANELLE RAINEY, PROGRAM DEVELOPMENT MANAGER

Date: January 22, 200—

Create name badges for conference presenters. Use the speaker data file (Job 3) for the merge information. Use WordArt for the name of the conference. Add a border around the name badge. Use a different font (but be sure it is large enough and easy to read by people approaching the speakers) for the presenter's name and company. Highlight the presenter's name. Include the SBI logo somewhere on the badge. Save as Job 23.

Name of Conference

Presenter's Name

Presenter's Company

SBI Logo

FEATURES: Highlight
Merge
Page Border
WordArt

S·B·I
SMALL BUSINESS INSTITUTE

FROM THE DESK OF JANELLE RAINEY, PROGRAM DEVELOPMENT MANAGER

Date: January 22, 200—
Create signs for the two pre-conference workshops. Use landscape orientation, include the information shown here, and be sure the signs complement each other and the name badges you prepared as Job 23 in design and color. Use WordArt for the title, fill in the background with a texture, and use a fancy page border. Save the first sign as Job 24a and the second as Job 24b.

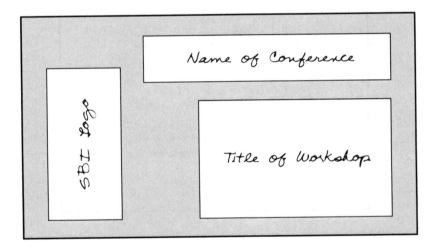

2714 SPRING FOREST ROAD • RALEIGH, NC 27610-1997 • (919) 555-0126

FEATURES: Clip Art
Fill
Grouping Objects
Page Border
Rotate Text
Text Box
WordArt

S·B·I
SMALL BUSINESS INSTITUTE

FROM THE DESK OF JANELLE RAINEY, PROGRAM DEVELOPMENT MANAGER

Date: January 22, 200–

Please prepare certificates of appreciation for the workshop presenters for the "E-Commerce and the New Economy" Conference and Exposition. Use a design and colors that complement the name badges and workshop signs. Merge the data file (Job 3) and print one certificate for me to look at. Be sure to include the SBI logo. Save the file as Job 25.

The certificate should contain all of the information that follows.

Certificate of Appreciation
presented to
[Presenter's Name]
for participation in
E-Commerce and the New Economy
Conference and Exposition
SBI Logo

_____   _____
Elijah J. Roberts, Director   Date

2714 SPRING FOREST ROAD • RALEIGH, NC 27610-1997 • (919) 555-0126

FEATURES: Clip Art
Fonts
Mail Merge
Page Border
WordArt

SMALL BUSINESS INSTITUTE

FROM THE DESK OF MELINDA CHEVEZ, ADMINISTRATIVE ASSISTANT

January 22, 200-

Open Job 15 and prepare the contracts for the following teachers. Use the current date on each form. Save the filled-in forms as Job 26a and Job 26b.

Mrs. Patricia Haynes   SS: 234-32-0393
4579 E. Washington Street
Raleigh, NC 27604-1999
3 courses
Term: Spring
Salary: $45/credit
Special Conditions: Supervise at least two hours of lab time for students.
Microsoft Project, Code: CI016-01
8 lecture hours, 2 lab hours, 10 total
Crystal Report 8.5 Introduction, Code: Bio12-02
12 lecture hours, 8 lab hours, 20 total
Visio Professional Basics, Code: CI026-04
12 lecture hours, 8 lab hours, 20 total

Dr. Marian Alephs SS: 214-09-9383
567 Foster Circle
Raleigh, NC 27605-1988
1 course
Term: Spring
Salary $60/credit
No special conditions
A+ Certification
10 lecture hours, 5 lab hours, 15 total

2714 SPRING FOREST ROAD • RALEIGH, NC 27610-1997 • (919) 555-0126

FEATURES: Protected Form

S·B·I
SMALL BUSINESS INSTITUTE

FROM THE DESK OF JANELLE RAINEY, PROGRAM DEVELOPMENT MANAGER

January 23, 200–

Please retrieve the data file Checklist and format the document as a three-column flyer. Use WordArt for the title and add a page border. Justify the text in columns, turn hyphenation on, add a line between columns, and add the SBI logo. Change the bullets to something fancy but appropriate and vary the fonts to format the flyer attractively. Format the paragraphs with 3 points space after but be sure the flyer fits on one page.

Insert hyperlinks to the Microsoft Office sample templates Balance Sheet and Cash Flow Statement. Save the flyer as Job 27a, and then save it again as an html file, Job 27b.

ROAD • RALEIGH, NC 27610-1997 • (919) 555-0126

FEATURES: Borders and Shading
Bullets and Numbering
Columns with Lines
Fonts
Hyperlinks
Hyphenation
Justification
Save As
WordArt

Checklist, Balance Sheet, Cash Flow Statement

JOB 27   SBI Small Business Institute   **51**

S·B·I
SMALL BUSINESS INSTITUTE

FROM THE DESK OF MELINDA CHEVEZ, ADMINISTRATIVE ASSISTANT

January 24, 200-

We have decided to produce a three-column quarterly newsletter for our staff and members. The members' copies will be mailed to them with a copy of the quarterly report in a 9" x 12" envelope. Retrieve the data file Newsletter. Use 1" margins and add Volume 1, Issue 1, Spring, and the current year as part of the masthead.

Select appropriate graphic images, clip art, styles for headings, and symbols for paragraph markers. Number pages at the bottom center. I am attaching the information to be used for the newsletter. Delete the "Marketing Concept" section and replace it with an article on the upcoming E-Commerce conference. You are to compose this article.

Add a table of contents titled "In This Issue" to the first page. Add a box at the very end of the last page that contains this information: The SBI Quarterly is published four times per year. For additional information, please contact: Small Business Institute, 2714 Spring Forest Road, Raleigh, NC 27610-1997, Phone: (919) 555-0126, Fax: (919) 555-0127, E-mail: ospecialist@sbi.org.

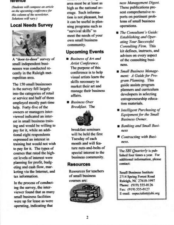

Newsletter

FEATURES: Columns
Bullets and Numbering
Graphics
Header and Footer
Line Spacing
Styles
Text Boxes

S·B·I
SMALL BUSINESS INSTITUTE

FROM THE DESK OF MELINDA CHEVEZ, ADMINISTRATIVE ASSISTANT

January 27, 200-

We need to prepare a news release for the upcoming Virtual Assistant Seminar. Use the following information to compose the news release.

The title of the seminar is "So You Want to be a VA." It will be held on Saturday, February 22, 200- at SBI from 9:00 a.m. until 12:00 p.m. The cost is $45.

The presenter of the workshop is Crystal Cohen, who has been a very successful virtual assistant for the past five years. She now provides training and resources for others who want to become virtual assistants.

The seminar will answer the question that is asked so often, "What is a virtual assistant?" It is designed to provide valuable information for persons who are interested in becoming virtual assistants as well as for persons who may be interested in using the services of a virtual assistant. Attendees will learn skills that will foster success in the virtual business.

To register for the seminar, call the Small Business Institute at (919) 555-0126.

2714 SPRING FOREST ROAD • RALEIGH, NC 27610-1997 • (919) 555-0126

FEATURES: Fonts
Line Spacing
Right Tabs

SMALL BUSINESS INSTITUTE

FROM THE DESK OF MELINDA CHEVEZ, ADMINISTRATIVE ASSISTANT

January 27, 200-

Retrieve the data file Signature Authority and replace the information in brackets with form fields. Add four signature and date lines at the end of the form. Align the signature lines at the left and the date lines at the right. Leave enough room between lines for people to sign and date the agreement. Add SBI as a diagonal watermark. Protect the form, and then fill it in with this information: Elijah Roberts is granting Janelle Rainey signature authority on his behalf for SBI in the amount of $15,000. Save the protected form as Job 30a. Save the filled-in form as Job 30b.

2714 SPRING FOREST ROAD • RALEIGH, NC 27610-1997 • (919) 555-0126

Signature Authority

FEATURES: Form Fields
Protected Form
Watermark

S·B·I
SMALL BUSINESS INSTITUTE

FROM THE DESK OF MELINDA CHEVEZ, ADMINISTRATIVE ASSISTANT

January 27, 200-

Write a memo to the staff to tell them that their evaluations will take place the week of March 15. Remind them to bring their self-evaluations to their evaluation sessions. Each member must schedule with me by March 1. Save this memo as Job 31a.

Write a congratulatory memo from Elijah to the staff on Cornell Fiazza's successful completion of her Microsoft Office Certification in Word, Excel, and Access at both the Core and Expert levels. Let her know how proud Elijah is and encourage her to continue to improve her skills. Please let everyone know that we will recognize Cornell at our annual service recognition award ceremony on February 12. Save this memo as Job 31b.

2714 SPRING FOREST ROAD • RALEIGH, NC 27610-1997 • (919) 555-0126

FEATURES: Memo Template
Spelling and Grammar

S·B·I
SMALL BUSINESS INSTITUTE

FROM THE DESK OF JANELLE RAINEY, PROGRAM DEVELOPMENT MANAGER

January 29, 200-

Please retrieve the pre-conference workshop handout (Job 1); then add the data file, Client Interest Form, as a second page following the handout, and save the file as a Web page named Job 32a.

Also add Job 12b and Job 27b to the Web page file and resave it as Job 32b.

2714 SPRING FOREST ROAD • RALEIGH, NC 27610-1997 • (919) 555-0126

Client Interest Form

FEATURES: Insert File
Save As

S·B·I
SMALL BUSINESS INSTITUTE

FROM THE DESK OF MELINDA CHEVEZ, *ADMINISTRATIVE ASSISTANT*

January 30, 200-

Please prepare the attached letter for Elijah's signature. The letter is to be sent to

Mr. Robert Ulrich, Program Manager
U. S. Small Business Administration
North Carolina District Office
6302 Fairview Road, Suite 300
Charlotte, NC 28210-4312

For each highlighted word, please use the Thesaurus to select another word. Proofread carefully and use the spelling and grammar checker.

Please edit the letter to keep the word count for the body to no more than about 375 words. Also, provide an envelope.

2714 SPRING FOREST ROAD • RALEIGH, NC 27610-1997 • (919) 555-0126

FEATURES: Header and Footer
Spelling and Grammar
Thesaurus
Word Count

It is with great pleasure that I submit this missive in support of the E-Commerce Small Business Initiative application for a U.S. Small Business Administration (SBA) grant, specifically for Program Announcement No. ECBO-3223-019.

It is our understanding that the proposal, if granted, will provide funding for five years to the Raleigh University Research and Technology Center (RURTC) District Area to provide counseling, training, and other technical assistance to small business owners who want to start or expand an e-commerce business. Mini-grants can be used to provide financial, management, marketing, loan, e-commerce, and government procurement/certification assistance.

As you can see, this proposal has delineated plans to set aside at least 10 percent of the total award for women business owners who are socially and economically disadvantaged in the target group and others who are veterans, have disabilities, are in agribusiness, are in home-based businesses, and those living in Empowerment Zones, rural and urban areas.

RURTC has cooperative agreement and grant with Charlotte Times Online to develop training materials for students in grades K-12. The E-Commerce grant funds will enhance the collaboration between institutions of higher education, the business community, K-12 schools, and technical service providers. The purpose of collaboration is to develop rigorous instructional materials, which employ information technologies and relevant newspaper-based data to enhance student understanding of entrepreneurship and the role of e-commerce in today's economy.

The number of applicants, with an anticipated minimum annual grant of $15,000, will determine agency awards. Directing funds as mini-grants will allow participating small businesses the flexibility to direct resources in ways that best facilitate and support implementation.

Charlotte Times Online is a valuable partner in the proposal because of its commitment to underwrite some of the professional development and development expenses critical to successful implementation. Further, the Times and RURTC will provide small businesses with an opportunity to share and publish their work, thus broadening the impact of entrepreneurship knowledge base.

We at the Small Business Institute strongly support the proposed initiative and see it as a great opportunity for all small businesses, agencies, and the larger educational community to collaborate in practical ways. Should this proposal be funded, SBI will certainly apply for a mini-grant. Providing service to small businesses is our top priority.

If you need additional information, please feel free to call me at (919) 555-0126 or e-mail me at eroberts@sbi.org.

SMALL BUSINESS INSTITUTE

FROM THE DESK OF MELINDA CHEVEZ, *ADMINISTRATIVE ASSISTANT*

Please compose a letter to the cleaning contractors expressing our displeasure with their work. Also include "INADEQUATE SERVICE" as the subject. You may cite the following:

All trash cans are not being emptied nightly.
Objects are not being moved so that dusting is complete.
Candy and other personal items are missing from offices.
Radios in offices are being played; stations are being changed.

Request that they improve their performance. If not, we will terminate our contract. Prepare the letter for my signature and provide an envelope.

Here's the contractor's address:

Mr. Joseph Knight
White Knight Cleaning Services
613 Oakside Crossing
Raleigh, NC 27613-1967

MC

2714 SPRING FOREST ROAD • RALEIGH, NC 27610-1997 • (919) 555-0126

S·B·I
SMALL BUSINESS INSTITUTE

FROM THE DESK OF MELINDA CHEVEZ, ADMINISTRATIVE ASSISTANT

January 30, 200-

Please key the attached outline in appropriate format. You will also need to proofread carefully. I did this in a hurry. Prepare a header for the second page that includes the title of the outline as well as the page number.

MC

2714 SPRING FOREST ROAD • RALEIGH, NC 27610-1997 • (919) 555-0126

FEATURES: Header and Footer
Tab Set

Sample Business Plan

I.   Cover Letter

     A.   Dollar amount required
     B.   Terms and timing
     C.   Type and price of securities

II. Summary

     A.   Business Description
          1.   Name
          2.   Location and plant description
          3.   Product
          4.   Market and competition
          5.   Management expertise
     B.   Business Goals
     C.   Summary of financial needs and application of funds
     D.   Earnings projections and potential return to investors

III. Market Analysis

     A.   Description of total market
     B.   Industry trends
     C.   Target market
     D.   Competition

IV. Products or Services

A.   Description of product line
B.   Proprietary position: patents, copyrights, and legal and technical
     considerations
C.   Comparison to competitors' products

V.   Manufacturing Process (if applicable)

     A.   Materials
     B.   Source of supply
     C.   Production methods

VI. Marketing Strategy

     A.   Overall strategy
     B.   Pricing policy
     C.   Method of selling, distributing, and servicing products

VII Management Plan

    A.   Form of business organization
    B.   Board of directors compostion
    C.   Officers: organization chart and responsibilities
    D.   Resumes of key personnel
    E.   Staffing plan/number of employees
    F.   Facilities plan/planned capital improvements
    G.   Operating plan/schedule of upcoming work for next one
        to two years

VII. Financial Data

    A.   Financial statements (five years to present)
    B.   Five-year financial projections (first year by quarters, remaining
        years annually)
        1.   Profit and loss statement
        2.   Balance sheets
        3.   Cash flow charts
        4.   Capital expenditure estimates
    C.   Explanation of projections
    D.   Key business ratios
    E.   Explanation of use and effect of new funds
    F.   Potential return to investors: comparison to average return in
        the industry as a whole

Use the data file Electronic Portfolio to create a resume and an electronic portfolio. Include those documents in this simulation that display a portfolio icon as sample projects in your portfolio.

Copy these files onto a CD and create a label for the CD. If possible, include a picture of yourself and an appropriate graphic image on the label.

Electronic Portfolio

Reference Manual

CERTIFICATE OF ATTENDANCE

presented

to

PETER W. WARREN

E-Commerce Conference

presented by

SBI: Small Business Institute

Raleigh, North Carolina

_____   _____

Elijah J. Roberts, Director   Date

ADDRESSING PROCEDURES

To automatically add the address of a displayed letter to an envelope, use the Envelopes and Labels feature. An alternative style for envelopes is upper case with no punctuation.

```
Small Business Institute
2714 Spring Forest Road
Raleigh, NC 27610-1997




                        Mr. Thomas Marshall
                        Gateway Enterprises
                        890 Summit Avenue
                        Raleigh, NC 27650-2003
```

Alternative format

```
SMALL BUSINESS INSTITUTE
2714 SPRING FOREST ROAD
RALEIGH NC 27610-1997




                        MR THOMAS MARSHALL
                        GATEWAY ENTERPRISES
                        890 SUMMIT AVENUE
                        RALEIGH NC 27650-2003
```

Use graphic elements such as clip art, borders, lines, WordArt, etc., when creating flyers. Vary the font style and size for special effects. Remember that flyers usually include larger fonts than a general publication.

A Workshop

on

FRANCHISING

is scheduled

for

Thursday, March 20, 200-

At the Raleigh Suites and Convention Center
2714 Spring Forest Road, Raleigh, NC 27609-1997
7:00–8:30 p.m.

Presented by Small Business Institute

S·B·I

SMALL BUSINESS INSTITUTE

2714 Spring Forest Road • Raleigh, NC 27610-1997 • (919) 555-0126 }   Letterhead

2" or
center
page

Current date   March 24, 200- ↓ 4

Letter address   Mr. Thomas Marshall
Gateway Enterprises
890 Summit Avenue
Raleigh, NC 27650-2003↓ 2

Salutation   Dear Mr. Marshall↓ 2

Body   The Small Business Institute cordially invites you to the E-Commerce Conference. This
event will feature a business exhibition, a series of informative workshops on e-
commerce, and a luncheon with distinguished speakers and local, successful
entrepreneurs. There will also be workshops on a relatively new career; that of the virtual
assistant. ↓ 2

Our annual conferences have been very successful in the past and we expect this year's
conference to surpass the others. Individuals from large and small businesses come
together, network, and learn from and about each other. ↓ 2

We sincerely hope that you can attend this event. You will leave with a wealth of new
information that would be very beneficial to your company. A registration form is
enclosed. ↓ 2

default side
margins

Sincerely↓ 4

Complimentary
closing

Name and
title   Elijah J. Roberts, Director↓ 2

Reference
initials   xx↓ 2

Enclosure
notation   Enclosure

Dr. John Warwick
Page 2
January 2, 200-

Header with name, page
number, and date

We will expect to have a reply to your inquiry as soon as we are able to investigate the matter more thoroughly. We would appreciate it if you would allow us sufficient time to do so. ↓2

Sincerely ↓4

Elijah J. Roberts, Director ↓2

xx ↓2

Enclosure

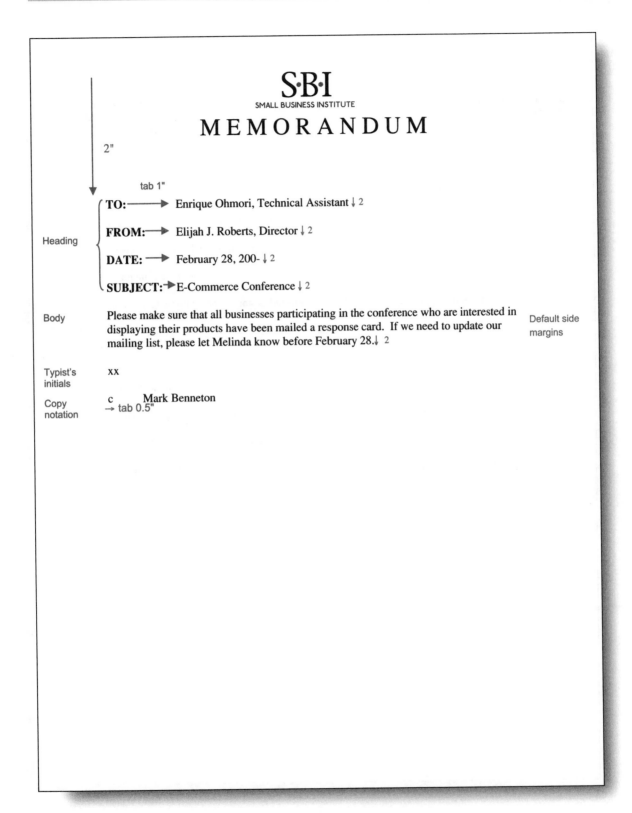

S·B·I

SMALL BUSINESS INSTITUTE

MEMORANDUM

2"

tab 1"

Heading

TO: → Enrique Ohmori, Technical Assistant ↓ 2

FROM: → Elijah J. Roberts, Director ↓ 2

DATE: → February 28, 200- ↓ 2

SUBJECT: → E-Commerce Conference ↓ 2

Body

Please make sure that all businesses participating in the conference who are interested in displaying their products have been mailed a response card. If we need to update our mailing list, please let Melinda know before February 28. ↓ 2

Default side margins

Typist's initials

xx

Copy notation

c   Mark Benneton
→ tab 0.5"

16 pt. Arial, underlined

<u>NEWS RELEASE</u>

SBI: Small Business Institute
2714 Spring Forest Road
Raleigh, North Carolina 27610-1997

12 pt. Arial right-aligned

↓2

Contact: Melinda Chevez ↓2

Phone: (919) 555-0126 ↓2

14 pt. bold and centered

FOR IMMEDIATE RELEASE ↓2

Bold

RALEIGH, NC, January 15, 200- — SBI: Small Business Institute has recently been awarded a $5,000,000 grant to be used to support new small businesses in the Raleigh area. The grant will be available to persons interested in starting new businesses. These monies have been earmarked for start-up costs such as equipment, building/office rental, software, and training.

Default side margins

SBI will host an information session for all interested prospective and new entrepreneurs in the Raleigh area who feel that they could benefit from this grant. The session will be held on Saturday, February 23, 200-, at 9:00 a.m. at SBI, which is located at 2714 Spring Forest Road in Raleigh. Call Melinda Chevez at (919) 555-0126 for sign-up information and directions. ↓2

###

Use columns to create newsletters. Use various font styles and sizes, lines, and graphics for special effects. A simple, uncluttered design with a significant amount of white space is recommended to enhance readability.

The SBI Quarterly

Volume II Issue II

Spring, 200-

HELP IS ON THE WAY!

If you need administrative help in your small business for a short amount of time or for a special project, a virtual assistant could be the help you need. A "VA" performs tasks such as word processing, desktop publishing, Internet research, spreadsheets—pretty much everything that a traditional administrative assistant does. What's the difference? The virtual assistant works from home. Many times, the business owner never sees the virtual assistant in person.

Another advantage to hiring a virtual assistant is that you will not have to withhold taxes or pay the VA benefits such as medical expenses, leave, retirement plan, or training.

SBI will present a workshop on the "Virtual Assistant" as part of its yearly conference. You won't want to miss it. Registration information will be sent to SBI members.

DO YOU WANT TO "REACH OUT AND TOUCH" MORE CUSTOMERS?

Learn to use the Internet to reach more customers. Make your business an e-commerce business. Get details on how to develop an e-business plan for your e-commerce business at the Raleigh Suites and Convention Center. Call (919) 555-0126 for more information.

FAMILY COOKOUT

The annual Family Cookout for all SBI members will be held at Lakewood Park on Saturday, May 23, 200-, from 12 noon. until 6 p.m. Each member is asked to pay $15 to assist with the cost of food. We hope that everyone will be able to join in the fun, food, games, and fellowship. Please call the office by May 15, 200-, to let us know if you will be attending and how many will be coming with you.

INSIDE THIS ISSUE

Making the Small Business Connection
Resources
Local Needs Survey
Upcoming Events

Set a decimal tab at .25" to align the roman numerals. Set left tabs at .5" and .75" to indent the subheads.

2"

BUSINESS RESOURCE CENTER ↓2

Title in 14 pt. bold

I.   TECHNICAL ASSISTANCE FOR THE COMMUNITY↓2

     A. Break-Even Analysis for Beginning Businesses
     B. Ration Analysis for Ongoing Businesses
     C. Forecasting for Businesses
        1. Advantages
        2. Examples
     D. Financial Statement Preparation↓2

II.   RESOURCE ASSISTANCE↓2

     A. Maintenance of Resources
        1. Library of SBA
        2. Other free publications
     B. List of Where to Go for Help↓2

III.   WORKSHOP SERIES↓2

     A. Financing a Business
     B. Loan Application Procedures
     C. Budget Preparation
     D. Automation Considerations

Proofreading Techniques

It is very important that all documents are error-free. Even though the software will automatically correct some errors and display some misspelled words and grammatical errors, it is necessary for you to proofread your document carefully. In addition to checking the document for errors, also be sure that document format is correct.

Follow these steps to ensure the accuracy of your documents:

■ Correct all errors displayed by the Spelling and Grammar check.

■ Scroll through the document to make sure that you have corrected all of the displayed errors.

■ Use Print Preview to view the entire document to ensure that all formatting is correct. Check margins, spacing, headings, paragraphs, headers, footers, page numbers, horizontal or vertical centering, and the overall appearance of the document.

■ Because proofreading documents on the screen can be difficult, print the document (double-spaced if possible).

■ Use a straight edge (i.e., a ruler or an envelope) to help keep your eyes focused on the correct line.

■ Read the document word for word. Pay special attention to proper names, correct word use (*cite*, *site*, or *sight*), punctuation, additions, and omissions. Sometimes it is helpful to read the lines backwards, from right to left.

■ Mark all errors using appropriate proofreaders' marks.

■ Correct all errors and save the document with the corrections.

PROOFREADERS' MARKS

Align ||	Insert space #
Bold ～～～	Let stand, ignore correction .... or *stet*
Capitalize ≡ or *Cap*	Lowercase / or *lc*
Center copy] [	Move down ⌊⌋
Close up ⌒	Move up ⌒
Delete ℓ	Move right]
Double space *DS*	Move left [
Insert ∧	Paragraph ¶
Insert apostrophe ∨'	Single space *ss*
Insert comma ∧	Spell out ○ *sp*
Insert period ⊙	Transpose ⌒ or *tr*
Insert quotation marks ∨ ∨	Underline or italics ___

2"

SEEKING ABUNDANCE AS AN ENTREPRENEUR

Title in 14 pt. bold

Default side margins

As an aspiring entrepreneur, I attended the "Seeking Abundance as an Entrepreneur" seminar hosted by Carla Gross. Mrs. Gross is the host of Financial Insight and is the author of *Smart Moves for the Female Entrepreneur*, which is a national best seller. (Banks, 2004, 25)

In her opening statement, Mrs. Gross reflected on a poem by Julio Torres entitled "Life Is Not a Bed of Roses." She said, "Her life has not been a bed of roses; instead, it has been filled with poverty and despair. However, after much determination, perspiration, and hard work, life is now filled with wealth, success, and prosperity; and it seems like a bed of roses."

"From poverty to wealth . . . from poverty to wealth," she stated over and over. She emphasized that it is simply amazing. Yet, she believes that anyone can do it if he or she has sheer determination, will power, perseverance, and the willingness to work hard.

Mrs. Gross definitely has joy. She was identified as one of the outstanding new entrepreneurs for 2003 by Minority Enterprise Magazine. (Mohanty, 2003, 89) Mrs. Gross' business is only six years old, but within that time she has increased her business worth from $150,000 to $3.5 million.

Mrs. Gross indicated that abundance can be interpreted to mean a state when you can do what you want to do and not have to worry about how. She further explained that

↑ at least 1" bottom margin

0.5"↓   2

1"▼ it takes approximately five to ten years to build up to that level and most individuals have

decided not to persevere that long in order to take advantage of abundance.

Steps to Abundance   bold

Mrs. Gross identified several basic steps for seeking abundance. The following is a summary, although not comprehensive, of her recommendations.

Create a plan. Write down your short- and long-range plans. Remember, this plan is only a guide. It can be changed, and it should be updated frequently. The following questions must be answered:

1. What?
2. Why?
3. When?
4. How?

Invest each pay day. Learn to pay yourself a little each pay period. The amount does not matter; consistency is the key. Once the routine has been established, increase the amount and the dividends will grow.

Own a home. Invest in a home. Don't let someone else benefit from your need for shelter. Your first home may not be your dream home, but it will be something that you own. You will be able to sell that home and probably get your dream home.

Invest in the stock market. Buy at least one share of some type of stock. If you buy one, you will buy more eventually. Read the financial sections of the newspaper.

Maximize your resources. Invest in yourself. You are the most valuable resource that you have. Stay current. Know what the latest trends and innovations are in your area. Read and attend workshops and seminars.

3

2"

REFERENCES ↓2   14 pt. bold

Use hanging
indent of 0.5"

Banks, Rochelle. *Smart Moves for the Female Entrepreneur*. 2d edition. Madison:
     Rainey Publishing Company, 2004. ↓2

Mohanty, Jarrod. "Outstanding New Entrepreneurs for 2003." *Minority Enterprise
     Magazine*. July, 2003.

2"

14 pt. bold, centered → **TABLE OF CONTENTS** ↓2

Default
side
margins

ii

Number with lowercase
Roman numeral

Center table vertically or DS before and after

SMALL BUSINESS INSTITUTE↓ 2		
Resources↓ 2		
Category	Number on Hand	Number Ordered
Books	36	8
Videos	21	13
CD-ROMs	14	45
Cassette Tapes	16	4
Laser Diskettes	2	20
Pamphlets	10	5
→0.5" Total	99	95

Heading centered in 14 pt. bold

Subheading centered in 12 pt. bold

Bold and → center

↑ right-align numbers ↑

Table with lines

SMALL BUSINESS INSTITUTE

Resources

Category	Number on Hand	Number Ordered
Books	36	8
Videos	21	13
CD-ROMs	14	45
Cassette Tapes	16	4
Laser Diskettes	2	20
Pamphlets	10	5
Total	99	95

Table without lines

Data files for completing various jobs are recorded on the CD in the back of this book or your instructor will make them available for your use. Open the data files and then save the file with the name of the job in which it will be used.

 This icon alerts you that a data file is needed to complete a specific job.

Balance Sheet (Excel)	Job 27
Cash Flow Statement (Excel)	Job 27
Chase Letter	Job 20
Checklist	Job 27
Client Interest Form	Job 32
Coaching Initiative	Job 22
Conference Registration	Job 5
Contacts (Access)	Job 6
Course Revenue	Job 10
Electronic Portfolio	Job 36
Evaluation Matrix	Job 18
Expense Report	Job 17
Interview Schedule	Job 19
Newsletter	Job 28
SBI Members (Access)	Job 16
Seminar Topics	Job 1
Signature Authority	Job 30
VA Certification (Excel)	Job 18

COMMAND SUMMARY

Command	Menu	Toolbar	Shortcut Keys
Align	Format/Paragraph		
AutoCorrect	Tools/AutoCorrect Options		
AutoFit	Table/AutoFit		
AutoSummarize	Tools/AutoSummarize		
AutoText	Tools/AutoCorrect Options		
Bold	Format/Font	**B**	Ctrl + B
Bookmarks	Insert/Bookmark		
Borders	Format/Borders and Shading		
Bullets and Numbering	Format Bullets and Numbering		
Center Page	File/Page Setup/Layout		
Change Case	Format/Change Case		
Character Effects/Styles	Format/Font		Ctrl + Shift + F
Clip Art	Insert/Picture/Clip Art		
Close	File/Close		
Columns	Format/Columns		
Comments	Insert/Comments		
Compare and Merge	Tools, Compare and Merge Documents		
Convert text to table	Table/Convert		
Copy	Edit/Copy		Ctrl + C
Cut	Edit/Cut		Ctrl + X
Date and Time	Insert/Date and Time		
Delete	Backspace or Delete Key		
Envelopes and Labels	Tools/Letters and Mailing		
Exit	File/Exit		Alt + F4
Fields	Insert/Field		
Fill	Format/Borders and Shading		
Find/Replace	Edit/Find/Replace		Ctrl + F; Ctrl + H
Font Size	Format/Font	11	Ctrl + Shift + > or <
Font Style	Format Font	Times New Roman	
Footnotes/Endnotes	Insert/Reference		
Form Fields	View/Toolbars/Forms		
Format Painter			
Forms Toolbar	View/Toolbars/Forms		
Formulas	Table/Formulas		
Graphics	Insert/Picture		
Header/Footer	View/Header and Footer		
Highlight			
Hyperlink	Insert/Hyperlink		Ctrl + K

Hyphenation	Tools/Language/Hyphenation		
Indent & Hanging Indent	Format/Paragraph		
Insert	Insert key		
Italic	Format/Font	*I*	Ctrl + I
Justification			
Labels and Envelopes	Tools/Letters and Mailings		
Line Spacing	Format/Paragraph		
Lines	Format/Borders and Shading		
Macros	Tools/Macro		
Mail Merge	Tools/Letters and Mailing		
Margins	File/Page Setup		
Merge Cells	Table/Merge Cells		
New	File/New		Ctrl + N
Object Order	Format/Object		
Open	File/Open		Ctrl + O
Outline	Format/Bullets and Numbering		
Page Border	Format/Borders and Shading		
Page Breaks	Insert/Break		Ctrl + Enter
Page Numbers	Insert/Page Numbers		
Page Orientation	File/Page Setup		
Paper Size	File/Page Setup		
Paragraph Styles	Format/Styles and Formatting	Normal + 11 pt	
Paste and Paste Special	Edit/Paste or Paste Special		Ctrl + V
Print	File/Print		Ctrl + P
Print Preview	File/Print/Print Preview		
Protect Document	Tools, Protect Document		
Readability	Tools/Word Count		
Rotate Text	Format/Text Direction		
Row Height	Table/Table Properties		
Ruler	View/Ruler		
Save	File/Save		Ctrl + S
Save As	File/Save As		F12
Shading	Format/Borders and Shading		
Show/Hide		¶	
Shrink to Fit	File/Page Setup		
Sort	Table/Sort		
Spelling and Grammar	Tools/Spelling and Grammar	ABC	F7
Split Cells	Table/Split Cells		

Styles	Format/Styles and Formatting	Normal + 11 pt	
Suppress Page Number	Insert/Page Numbers		
Table of Contents	Insert/Reference		
Tables	Table/Insert Table	⊞	
Tabs	Format/Tabs or Horizontal Ruler		
Template	File/New		
Text Boxes	Insert/Text Box		
Thesaurus	Tools/Language		Shift + F7
Track Changes	Tools/Track Changes		Ctrl + Shift + E
Underline	Format/Font	U	Ctrl + U
Undo/Redo	Edit/Undo or Redo	↺ ▾ ↻ ▾	Ctrl + Z; Ctrl + Y
Watermarks	Format/Background		
Web Pages	File/Save As		
Widow/Orphan	Format/Paragraph/Line and Page Breaks		
Word Art	Insert/Picture	𝐴	
Word Count	Tools/Word Count		
Zoom	View/Zoom/Full Page	▯	

Correlation of Microsoft Word 2003 Specialist Standards

	Skill Sets and Skills	Jobs
WW03S-1	**Creating Content**	
WW03S-1-1	Insert and edit text, symbols, and special characters	1, 11, 23, 24
WW03S-1-2	Insert frequently used and pre-defined text	4
WW03S-1-3	Navigate to specific content	22, 33
WW03S-1-4	Insert, position, and size graphics	2, 5
WW03S-1-5	Create and modify diagrams and charts	2
WW03S-1-6	Locate, select, and insert supporting information	13
WW03S-2	**Organizing Content**	
WW03S-2-1	Insert and modify tables	3, 6, 9, 10, 15, 17
WW03S-2-2	Create bulleted lists, numbered lists, and outlines	11, 13, 14
WW03S-2-3	Insert and modify hyperlinks	12, 27
WW03S-3	**Formatting Content**	
WW03S-3-1	Format text	1, 2, 18, 19
WW03S-3-2	Format paragraphs	1, 2, 11, 12, 13, 15, 22
WW03S-3-3	Apply and format columns	16, 27, 28
WW03S-3-4	Insert and modify content in headers and footers	16, 18, 22
WW03S-3-5	Modify document layout and page setup	1, 3, 5, 8, 11, 16, 17
WW03S-4	**Collaborating**	
WW03S-4-1	Circulate documents for review	
WW03S-4-2	Compare and merge document versions	6, 22
WW03S-4-3	Insert, view, and edit comments	20
WW03S-4-4	Track, accept, and reject proposed changes	20
WW03-5	**Formatting and Managing Documents**	
WW03-5-1	Create new documents using templates	4, 21, 31
WW03-5-2	Review and modify document properties	33
WW03-5-3	Organize documents using file folders	4, 6, 18
WW03-5-4	Save document in appropriate formats for different uses	4
WW03-5-5	Print documents, envelopes, and labels	7, 14, 20, 21, 23, 25, 26, 27, 28, 33
WW03-5-6	Preview documents and Web pages	1, 32
WW03-5-7	Change and organize document views and windows	

	Skill Sets and Skills	Jobs
WW03E-1	**Formatting Content**	
WW03E-1-1	Create custom styles for text, tables, and lists	
WW03E-1-2	Control pagination	1
WW03E-1-3	Format, position, and resize graphics using advanced layout features	2, 5, 15
WW03E-1-4	Insert and modify objects	
WW03E-1-5	Create and modify diagrams and charts using data from other sources	16
WW03E-2	**Organizing Content**	
WW03E-2-1	Sort content in lists and tables	1, 3, 6
WW03E-2-2	Perform calculations in tables	10, 17
WW03E-2-3	Modify table formats	3, 6, 8, 9, 10, 19
WW03E-2-4	Summarize document content using automated tools	22, 33
WW03E-2-5	Use automated tools for document navigation	
WW03E-2-6	Merge letters with other data sources	7
WW03E-2-7	Merge labels with other data sources	7, 16, 21, 23, 24, 25
WW03E-2-8	Structure documents using XML	
WW03E-3	**Formatting Documents**	
WW03E-3-1	Create and modify forms	8, 15, 26, 30
WW03E-3-2	Create and modify document background	8, 22, 30
WW03E-3-3	Create and modify document indexes and tables	
WW03E-3-4	Insert and modify endnotes, footnotes, captions, and cross references	11, 18
WW03E-3-5	Create and manage master documents and subdocuments	
WW03E-4	**Collaborating**	
WW03E-4-1	Modify track changes options	20
WW03E-4-2	Publish and edit Web documents in Word	32
WW03E-4-3	Manage document versions	22
WW03E-4-4	Protect and restrict forms and documents	30
WW03E-4-5	Attach digital signatures to documents	
WW03E-4-6	Customize document properties	
WW03E-5	**Customizing Word**	
WW03E-5-1	Create, edit, and run macros	4, 14
WW03E-5-2	Customize menus and toolbars	
WW03E-5-3	Modify Word default settings	4

Job Log

Job No.	Date Completed	Grade	Comments
1			
2			
3			
4			
5			
6			
7			
8			
9			
10			
11			
12			
13			
14			
15			
16			
17			
18			
19			
20			
21			
22			
23			
24			
25			
26			
27			
28			
29			
30			
31			
32			
33			
34			
35			
36			